Who You Really Are

Gail Alexander

PEN & PUBLISH

Saint Louis, Missouri

Published by

St. Louis, Missouri
(314) 827-6567
info@PenandPublish.com
www.PenandPublish.com

Print ISBN: 978-1-956897-77-7
ebook ISBN: 978-1-956897-78-4
Library of Congress Control Number: 2025947914

This book is printed on the USA on acid-free paper.

Dedication

Thank you to all who are walking their paths, sharing their light and being who you are really meant to be.

Thank you to all who believe in me and let me help guide your path.

Thank you, Kerry, for the amazing foreword.

Thank you to Brenda for the assist with grammar.

Thank you, Julie G, Sue K and Nate S, for the quotes for the back cover.

Contents

Foreword

I read Gail Alexander's *Who You Really Are* in one sitting, one hour and thirty-five minutes, to be precise, and I could not put it down. From the first page Gail does something rare: she speaks directly to the parts of us that have been waiting to be seen. In a few clear, luminous passages, she holds history and mystery side by side, Atlantis, Egypt, the times of Jesus, the many portals of our planet, and makes the cosmic feel intimate and possible.

Gail is an intuitive, and she treats intuition not as a curiosity but as a practical, everyday tool. The mandalas and images she creates are designed to do the same thing: act as keys. The universal language of symbol and sacred geometry appears again and again in this book because symbols translate the language of the energy field into something our minds and hearts can hold. When a book awakens recognition, it's more than agreeing with ideas; it's being reflected. Gail's voice met me there. I found myself sitting with memories and questions I've carried for years, the figures and guides who visit me, past-life echoes from Egypt that affected my voice, the horses and unicorns that show up as guardians of joy, and the steady presence of the Collective and Gaia.

I told Gail last night, **"I felt like I was seen for the first time while reading this book."** That feeling matters. It is what turns information into healing.

Who You Really Are is not a catalogue of beliefs; it's an invitation. Gail doesn't simply narrate channeled messages; she translates them. She gives the reader practical footholds: questions to reflect on, gentle exercises, and images that lift the reader into recognizing their own multidimensional nature. Whether you come to these pages as a skeptic, a seeker, or someone simply tired and hungry for more, you'll find a steadying hand and an open heart.

There is courage here. Gail names the shadows as readily as she celebrates the light. She speaks of mistakes made in other lifetimes and the tender work of forgiveness; she reminds us that time is layered and that our healing often asks us to change perspective rather than outcomes. Woven throughout is a warmth and humor that makes even the greatest mysteries feel like a conversation over tea.

If you allow it, this book will do two things at once: expand your sense of what's possible and root you in the simple power of your present life. It will nudge you to trust your own guidance, to notice the beings who help you, and to remember that your life, in all its ordinary and extraordinary moments, matters to the whole.

Thank you, Gail, for writing with humility, authority, and that rare quality of a true witness. To the reader: keep a pen nearby. You will want to underline, circle, and return to these pages again and again.

With love and trust,

Kerry Muller
www.thesubliminalself.com

Introduction

This book is an explanation of what you believe to be possible in human form. Who you really are as human beings is about connection, soul, light and love. Each and every one of you is an aspect of the divine and carries your own individual frequency and energy.

We wish for humanity to untether itself from its current beliefs about what is possible and instead follow its heart and trust its intuition. Every day is an opportunity for growth, movement, and living in the flow. All is as it is meant to be. Control and power are illusions created to keep humanity stuck in a loop.

This was discussed in my last book, *Wakey-Wakey, It's Time! Humanity, Pay Attention*. It is time and imperative to break free and be. You are light beings living in a human suit of three-dimensional energy at the present moment. Human beings are capable of magnificence beyond your human capacity to understand. Embark on this journey with us and discover who you really are meant to be.

This one who is transcribing and channeling us has had many different experiences we will use as a point of reference so you can understand more easily. Trust your gut, knowingness, senses, messages and signs. Settle in. We are here to help stretch you, guide you and prepare you for the next phase of human existence.

"Buckle up, Buttercup." We love sharing that saying because it makes this one laugh, and laughter helps raise the vibration, which is why there is a lot of humor in how we come across to this one. We wish to guide you during this time of transformation. Some may use the word *upheaval*; we prefer *transformation* or *enlightenment*, as it is a choice. You are more capable than you know.

There will be many teachers who will come through. We each have different energy signatures, which will resonate differently with each of you. Ready to take the next step? Let's go!

We will identify who we are as we come through. Sometimes it will be a singular being, sometimes the Collective, and sometimes just groups, like in this section.

We look forward to sharing this space and time with you.

Let the journey begin!

Archangel Azrael and Archangel Ariel

Section One:
Places

Atlantis

For me, Atlantis was the beginning of my spiritual journey here on Earth. I am an angel who volunteered to come down to help humankind. I am not sure what I was thinking at the time because coming to Earth means having free will. At this time when the Angels came down, we still had all of our abilities and capabilities. This will make more sense when we get to the Egypt chapter, which is next. I was very connected to Archangel Metatron in my Atlantean lifetime, and he is helping me co-write this section.

At the end of Atlantis, many of us knew what was coming and took the information and put it in various places on Earth and in the Cosmos for safekeeping. This is more detailed in my book, *I Still Know What I Know*. There were a select few who made promises to keep this information safe and protected until it would be time to share with humanity again.

My love for crystals comes from this time and how we harnessed the power and knowledge of crystals to help Atlantean society run. I have enough crystals now to open my own crystal store. There are times I will sit down and make grids to hold certain energies and frequencies for the planet. At the beginning of my journey, I was on a quest to recreate the gateway to Atlantis with 144 spheres. I probably have enough spheres to do it now.

I don't know about you, but when I go to buy crystals, they talk to me, or I am unable to put them down. I can read them and give you the information from them. I am also really good at picking crystals for other people as to what they need to work with at that time.

My favorite crystal is Labradorite; you can never have too much. My favorite combination for grids and helping with negativity is selenite, black tourmaline, and rose quartz, balancing light, dark and love.

When I first moved into the building I currently live in, my unit was right across from the elevators. There was so much energy in my apartment from myself and all the crystals that I kept shorting out the elevators. In the beginning, it made me laugh, but as time went on, it was not as funny. So, I created a grid to balance the energies, and everything now works harmoniously, except for normal elevator troubles.

Many of us have had these kinds of experiences but sometimes just don't put two and two together how our energy can affect everything around us and vice versa.

In the beginning when all my gifts and abilities were coming back online, I used to blow light bulbs in my house and streetlamps when I would drive by. When touch screen phones came out, I blew through three in a few weeks until I could find one that worked within my energy field. I would drain watch batteries every month; they are meant to last longer. I also cracked a band of a ring in half. The jeweler asked me what was going on, as this was not normal.

For me, it was learning to balance my energy and frequency with my environment around me. This took quite a while to accomplish. As we wake up and remember who we really are, our vibration changes, our lives change and we need to learn to balance all of it with our environment. I share a couple of these stories as it is important to remember there is nothing wrong with you; you are just leveling up.

I believe this is why I love movies about Atlantis, like *Aquaman*, because there is an element of the truth we are trying to uncover and the power that existed. There needs to be a balance between power, consciousness, spirit, light and soul, and this became out of balance for Atlantis. When used in balance and consciously, we flourished, thrived and expanded. At the end, Atlanteans pushed the confines of what is possible in experimentation without consciousness, which led to the downfall.

Have you ever heard the expression about opening Pandora's box? That is what a faction of Atlanteans did; they opened Pandora's box and then it could not be closed. This faction ended up destroying their own civilization in the process. By the time they realized the damage they were doing, it was too late.

As human beings, we are not ready yet to remember this power due to the state of affairs and choices being made on the Earth right now. There will be a time when we will remember, and our DNA will be unlocked.

In the end Atlantis was transformed to a different frequency and vibration. We are fascinated by what came before our current incarnation of mankind because, on a cellular level, it is encoded, we know it existed, and we're trying to find answers.

Many still carry this imprint of Atlantis and are trying to bring forth some of the best parts to humanity now. This is why it is said that Atlantis is rising, not the continent, but the consciousness.

I needed to share this part of my journey before I get to Egypt. Thank you, Archangel Metatron, for bringing forth this knowledge, insight, and understanding.

Questions:

Do you resonate with crystals?

Do you feel connected to Atlantis?

Have you ever had glimpses or feelings surrounding Atlantis?

Egypt

I have always been fascinated by Egypt and for a long time wanted to study archeology to help uncover the truth, the knowledge and wisdom we have been entrusted with at different times of our existence.

I have always known that I have had lifetimes in Egypt and have done some not-so-good things. It is only recently that I have known the extent of what I did in one lifetime and how it has affected the rest of my human lifetimes. I have always joked around that Earth is a reality show for other beings, and it turns out, it was for me. I will explain. As I said in the Atlantis section, I am an angel who came to help humanity and was walking amongst humans in this lifetime to help civilization move forward. This will be important because even being an angel on Earth, I had free will.

I was very frustrated with the choices that human beings were making and was not going to live through another civilization destroying itself like I had to watch with Atlantis, Lemuria, Mu, etc. So, this is the not-so-good part. Human beings were starting to misuse power again, just like in Atlantis, and I could not bear to go through this again. Apparently, with my angel abilities, I created a great flood and wiped out the people who were abusing their power; unfortunately, I also wiped out many other innocent bystanders and fellow angels as well. This is beginning to sound like a made-for-TV movie, I know, and this is what I have been shown.

The consequence of my actions was that I was placed in Angel Time-Out, so to speak, for what would be an equivalent of 1000 Earth years. During this time, I watched humanity like a reality show, learning the patterns, decisions and choices so that when I was given permission to return to Earth, I would not do it again. This is the simplistic version of everything that happened. There is so much more I could say, and it is not relevant to the story at this time.

I had always felt like I had seen the earth from above and had a connection to everything that has gone on and not known why until the memory above surfaced. I am a record keeper of sorts; it is part of my job to help guide humanity, not judge or interfere again, just guide and hold space. I was sent back at this time during these transitions to work with humanity to ascend into who you really are and what you are capable of doing.

In my first two books, *I Don't Know How I Know . . . I Just Know* and *I Still Know What I Know*, I go into more detail about my healing experiences and the Priestesses of ISIS. In my book *Wakey-Wakey, It's Time! Humanity, Pay Attention* I channeled a healing meditation, taking you to the healing pyramid from Egypt.

I remember going crystal shopping one time. I was playing with the clear quartz crystals, put three of them together, and then took a step back. I had recreated the crystals in a smaller scale that were on the altar in the Healing Temple in Egypt. Sometimes, we are not always aware of why we are doing some of the things we are doing. They all have meaning and importance for our soul's growth and development.

I have always had an aversion to crystal skulls until I was instructed to purchase 13 crystal skulls and recreate the grid. I did accomplish this and then was downloaded with more information about the universe, Earth, and why we are here.

At times I find myself getting frustrated with the choices and decisions made by humanity in our current times. I know that I am not going to do anything to hurt mankind this time. I learned my lesson. I am here as a resource and to support. I guess this is why I have so many gifts and abilities. Now, I just need to choose wisely. In the movie *Finding Nemo*, the shark says that fish are friends, not food. My new saying is humanity is friend, not a foe; do not hurt, help. Then when the fish are trapped in the net, they say to keep on swimming, swimming, swimming. That is what we need to do as human beings; we need to keep on swimming and moving forward. We have been here before and it is up to all of us to keep the human race moving forward, evolving and transforming.

If I have learned anything from my time observing Earth and mankind, it is that there are always patterns, choices, decisions, movement forward and backward. It is time for the human race to understand what you are really capable of doing in love, consciousness and in alignment with the laws of the universe.

Thank you to Archangel Metatron and Archangel Azrael for guiding me, teaching me and forgiving me as I wrote this section.

Questions:

Have you ever felt called to study, watch documentaries, or read about Egypt?

Do you have a sense of knowing or a feeling like you were there?

Can you let go of past mistakes?

Times of Jesus

I always wondered why I had such a strong connection to Jesus and felt like when He walked the earth, I was observing it. Why? Because as explained in the previous section, I was studying, paying attention, and taking notes while I was in detention, so when given the chance to come back again, I could reintroduce all of these teachings when the time was right.

Jesus was a teacher, a Master, not a religious figure. He was made into that by man to control us and keep us stuck in a paradigm that does not need to exist. I talk about my experiences with Jesus more formally in my book *Jesus and the Jewish Girl*.

Jesus is also known as Jeshua and Christ Consciousness. To let you in on a little secret, the Earth Mother, Gaia, is Christ Consciousness. The Earth is seeded with the golden energy of the Christ light. This is why all of us humans are capable of so much more. Remember, I said Jesus was a teacher; this is what he was here to teach, what being in a human suit can really do. We have forgotten. It is time to remember. When what we call miracles happen, it is because they are in alignment with the divine, and this allows the greatness we carry to come through for a brief moment.

Many forces here on Earth do not wish to awaken to the Christ consciousness of the planet and within. It makes me think about the scene from Avatar by the great tree, where they are all connected and there is this white light that covers all of them. We are capable of Earth being this way if we are open to challenging very old-standing beliefs.

The other day, I was getting a lecture on the Bible from my spirit team. Who wrote the Bible? Men, the patriarchy, wrote it as a form of control and manipulation. Like I said in *Jesus and the Jewish Girl*, the cross was the symbol for white light and was taken and then put on churches as a way to control us. There is no reason that each and every person cannot have their own relationship with the divine; individuals do not need to go through anyone else. That is the difference between religion and spirituality. We are all capable; we all possess the ability to go within and connect, like in Avatar. We have lost our faith along the way, our belief that anything is possible and our knowledge of who we really are.

There is more power, love, light and laughter when we all work together than when we are separated and fighting each other. Think about that. That is the paradigm that has been created on Earth. This is the paradigm that needs to shift as more and more awaken. Our DNA is re-awakening and calling for us to remember who we are.

Thank you, Jesus, Archangel Metatron, Archangel Uriel and Archangel Azrael for these reminders.

Questions:

Have you felt connected to the times of Jesus?

Do you feel connected to the Christos Consciousness?

Do you believe miracles are possible?

Do you believe we all have healing abilities?

Antarctica

A few months ago, I was directed to watch everything I could find on Antarctica and, of course, did not understand why at the time. Antarctica is regularly in my dreams, and I travel there multidimensionally often. Part of my role on Earth at this time is to protect all the crystals and grids on and around the Earth. I share more about this in my book, *I Still Know What I Know*, about the control panel I have been given to complete this work.

Antarctica is a multidimensional portal or gateway that has been hidden for a long time due to the terrain. We as humans are fascinated by that which we do not understand. As this one knows, Antarctica's portal was designed to keep Earth moving forward, regardless of what humanity chooses. This is why it is now being visited and explored. Humans are craving the truth, knowledge, wisdom and understanding of what their true role is in the cosmos and universe. Humanity wants to know its origins, who we really are and why we are here.

If you have been called to go to Antarctica, this is why. Many are ready to remember that we are multidimensional beings and ready to awaken to this fact. Trust your intuition, nudges, guidance and knowing it will serve you well. Part of the shift and what happens when you go to Antarctica is that there is no outside noise. You are forced to go inward, trusting and relying on others and yourself. It is an undiscovered wonderland just like our oceans. It is really important to see that you are multidimensionally connected and one with everything that surrounds us. Antarctica provides this experience, as do other sacred places around the globe.

Each human being is also a wonderland of knowledge, a spark of the divine and a spark of the Earth learning to co-exist harmoniously.

There is more than one multidimensional hub on Earth hiding in plain sight. This is why so many are drawn to what you call sacred places: Stonehenge, Glastonbury, Sedona, sacred sites in India, France, Mexico, the Camino, etc. This is why, as humans, you make sacred pilgrimages. Wake up! We need you to be who you really are. We need you to be the conscious living multidimensional light beings in a human suit you are.

Who is ready? We are here to assist and help those who are brave enough to challenge the current paradigm or game. Let's go! It's Time. What is at stake in the universe is more than just humanity's sovereignty.

This section was brought to you by Archangel Metatron and Melchizedek.

Questions:

Do you feel pulled to learn about Antarctica?

Do you feel déjà vu while watching shows about or reading about Antarctica?

Do you feel like there is a part of you there or do you have a knowingness about Antarctica?

Pilgrimages

All pilgrimages are unique to each soul. Some are physical, where you travel to an actual place and walk in that space, taking in all the energy, vibration and knowledge, as there may be parts of yourself left from past lives that need to be recovered. Some pilgrimages are psychological with what you need to work through to free your mind. Some are related to the human body and working through a dis-ease. Some are metaphysical and multidimensional. Whatever your own unique pilgrimage is, it is exactly what your soul needs to evolve.

There is no need to compare, as we are on our own unique journey together. Trust you are being led to whatever you need to continue your soul's evolution.

I have had several physical pilgrimages; the biggest one was to Ireland toward the beginning of my odyssey into my gifts and abilities.

Let's take my trip to Ireland, for example. The only place I wanted to go was New Grange. I skipped the explanation and was waiting in line so I could be the first to go in. I started to walk in, and I got extremely nauseous and dizzy. An invisible wall blocked me from moving forward. I heard my spirit team say I had to leave; I was not permitted to enter. I was crushed. So, while the whole party I went with was able to tour it, I walked around the perimeter. My spirit team told me I was not allowed to walk in on myself, which was why I was not permitted in. I understood much later that I was existing multidimensionally and part of me was currently there and was not allowed to walk in on myself. That would have affected many timelines.

My whole trip to Ireland was kind of a blur. I remember landing in Shannon and leaving from Dublin; the in-between part, not so much. I do remember being in the van we rented, and as we drove across the country, I remember seeding the country with energy. I remember my hands moving, and I was not really sure what I was doing at the time. This has always stuck with me for some reason. I did not have much luck going into all the haunted castles. Every time I went into one, my body temperature would drop. It got to the point I was wearing three pairs of socks, two pairs of pants, a hat and gloves and still could make it more than 20 minutes. I would just go wait in the van for the rest of my party. Again, each person's experiences are different, and at the same time, we have all had things happen that we cannot explain at the time. Reflection helps to make sense later.

The next physical pilgrimage was to Sedona. I rented a car and drove from Phoenix to Sedona. I remember driving down the hill and having an AHA moment. The thought that popped into my head is that each vortex is an energy center that correlates to the human energy field. The next thought took me aback as my spirit team said this is the mothership. I did not understand that at the time.

I signed up for a private tour, and others ended up coming. Other than the tour guide driving us to the places, I was the one who gave the tour. I explained all the vortexes we visited and all the feelings, energy, etc. So glad I paid for a tour I ended up giving... LOL.

I remember going into a crystal store after hiking one day and having my aura photo taken. Let me just say that all the salespeople in the store were ignoring me until after they saw my aura photo. Then they all came running up to me as my entire aura was indigo blue, and they had never seen that before. I hadn't changed, they ignored me, then all of a sudden, they were all swarming around me. It is interesting how things can change when we get new pieces of information.

I have had many metaphysical pilgrimages. In meditations, dreams or chanting, I have been taken to India, the sacred temple in Tibet, had a tea ceremony with Jesus, Kuan Yin and Buddha, as I have talked about in previous books.

Trust that you are taken and guided to where you need to go and to have the experiences you need to have. Our inclination is to compare our journey to others around us. Take your journey and have your experiences. This is what is important. I share to give you seeds to think about for yourself.

Questions:

Have you ever been pulled to a physical place?

What did that feel like for you?

Have you ever traveled in your dreams or meditations and instantly felt at home?

Section Two:

Experiences and Wisdom

Where Do We Go from Here?

This section is being written in harmony with the messages from The Pleiadeans. Humanity, you have a choice as to what happens next. Humanity was designed to be the bridge between the Cosmos and All That Is while being in a physical human suit and on the planet of free will.

How do you move forward? This is the choice, dilemma, or issue at hand; different words will resonate with different beings reading this, so we used several. Pick the one that feels right for you. They are laughing, showing me the pick-your-own-adventure books because that is what life on Earth is. Pick your own adventure and commit.

As we have said before, you are more capable than you know. You are caught in an illusion that you are not as powerful as a way to control and manipulate you. Like in the TV series *Discovery of Witches*, you have all been spellbound and need to be opened up and freed.

It is always interesting to me when I am directed to watch certain movies or TV shows, read books, or listen to certain songs. If you can let go and trust that the pieces of the puzzle will unfold in front of you, it makes life an interesting journey. Sometimes, you struggle to see the possibilities because you have been taught to limit yourselves. Oftentimes, you just see with your physical eyes and therefore do not get the whole picture. All dimensions and time happen simultaneously, and if you only look through your physical senses, there is so much you miss. We need for mankind to think bigger, to think multidimensionally. We need mankind to start playing the long game while also being in the present moment. This is possible as it is just a shift in perspective and awareness. This is where human consciousness is meant to be at this time. This is Who You Really Are!

Welcome to your seat at the cosmic or universal table. We have been waiting for you. Please take your seat; you are needed at this time.

This one channeling is doing everything in her ability to help facilitate this shift. With every mandala/portal she has been creating for the last 25 years, she has been bringing the frequency up, as have others scattered around the earth. This is why so many resonate with her images as they are a bridge to help unlock All That Is.

We need humanity to start to take a higher view of yourselves and your home. There is more to see and be. We need you to get out of your heads or intellect and into your heart and guts, sensing and knowing. We need you to be able to do this because when all is said and done, you are a multidimensional light being/soul in a human suit. You were instructed from childhood to think that you are only having a human experience and that is what is important. This is not true. Being on Earth and in a human suit is about having a multidimensional experience, blending light, wisdom, soul growth, knowledge and love. You are more than what you think, which leads to this one's previous book, *Wakey-Wakey, It's Time!*

The rest of your lineage, by lineage we mean light beings, angels and ascended masters. We chose that word intentionally and are waiting patiently, trying to help, guide and support you on this journey. Break the shackles, leave the illusion.

Many are caught up in the politics of the world right now. and this is a way to control the masses by being so focused on this, you are missing what is beyond this. We are going to repeat it, learning to see multidimensionally and the big picture while also affecting change in the present moment. Break free, it is your time to shine and take your place.

Questions:

Where do you see yourself going?

Where do you feel humanity is going?

Do you trust yourself and what you know?

Healing Abilities

This section was written in collaboration with Archangel Raphael and Archangel Metatron.

At the beginning of my spiritual development, I took many different healing classes. I was trying to have the background to validate what I could already do. I did not trust myself at this time and thought more classes would make me more legitimate.

Each class I took, about two hours into the class, I would understand the methods, how to use them and what they were for. I do not know how many teachers were annoyed with me because I was in the class, and they told me I already knew how to do it. The problem was that I was not yet conscious of everything I could do in this lifetime. I would get discouraged and upset each time a teacher told me this. I started to believe there was something wrong with me instead of seeing the gifts that I had. It took me many years, just like others reading this, to see that I was exactly as I was meant to be. I was awake and not asleep and did not fit into the mold they were desperately trying to force me into.

One of the things my spirit team told me in the beginning was that each healing technique held a different frequency and vibration, and I wanted to learn as many as I could so I could hold all those frequencies to help others.

One of the most important things I learned at this time was to trust that I would be shown or would know what to do. Sometimes I would just let my hands go where they needed to go. We all have this sense; sometimes we just don't pay attention to it. I was always guided; I was never in my ego or attached to the outcome. I would often see white light shooting out my hands, sometimes rainbow light. I could easily see the blockages in people's physical body and auric fields. As I have shared previously, it was like seeing people in a CAT scan machine, and the blockages or areas of dis-ease would light up.

The lesson they want us to learn is to trust ourselves. We are always guided and supported by the seen and unseen forces. Call on your guides, angels, teachers, loved ones, arch angels, ascended masters and light beings. Learn who you work with, so you know who is coming through.

At the beginning of my journey 25 years ago, I was given information that sound, frequency and vibration were all we needed to heal. This is now becoming a reality. We need to learn to think outside the box, as there really is no box at all; it is an illusion. I was also shown devices to detect and heal genetic disorders; a light scope would be the best way to talk about it. I never knew what I was supposed to do with this information until now. I am just supposed to plant the seeds; it is all being created and invented as I write this.

In the beginning of my journey, which I like to refer to as Mr. Toad's Wild Ride on Acid because that is what it felt like, I got download after download. At the beginning, it was a lot of medical information. I was shown DNA, how it moves, the patterns it forms, how it interacts, how to heal it, and the colors it changes depending on illness. Here we are today at the precipice of starting to understand that everything is not always as it appears and that spirituality is an important part of the healing journey. Traditional medicine right now treats illness or dis-ease in the body. We are capable of healing the meat suit.

I am also reminded while I write this section of all the times the dolphins and whales have come in and shown me how to heal, taking time and space into consideration. Dolphins and whales use sound, resonance and echo location. They know where they are at all times. Dolphins have an amazing ability to help humans heal. Remember, we have free will. Sometimes illness or dis-eases come back after being healed, as the thought process has not shifted to hold the frequency of the healing. There is so much that we still need to learn and understand. We can heal with sound, frequency and vibration; it involves shifting the paradigm and thinking multidimensionally. You see, we are a light being, a soul, and a human being. Healing involves treating all layers together, not just the human or meat suit, which is what we seem to be focused on. There is a difference in healing and treating and maybe it is time we start to look at what we are really doing.

I don't know about you, but when I was growing up, my pediatrician 's office had two waiting rooms: a healthy one and a sick one. It was quite the dilemma when one of your children was ill and the other one was healthy. Looking back on it now, I ask myself what kind of message did that send? A sick waiting room does not bode well for recovery. It's just interesting when you look back on things and what pops in. These messages and beliefs have shaped us and how we see medicine today. Eastern and Western medicine are both important as again you are not treating just the meat suit.

I was also thinking about how my doctor spends maybe 15 minutes with me. How do you build rapport and trust and how does that help heal? Medicine, to me, feels like a business of just treating symptoms, not the whole person, body, mind and spirit. I am not sure why I am including this, and with that said, maybe we need to take a step back. What is really in our best interest? Fifteen minutes, a prescription and that will help everything. Again, we are more than just the meat suit, which western medicine may help, but what about the mind, spirit, soul, etheric field, etc.?

Questions:

Do people feel better after they spend time with you?

Do you ever get a tingling or hot/cold sensation in your hands?

Have you ever had an awareness after talking to someone about what they are struggling with?

Time

This section is brought to you by Archangel Ariel and Melchizedek. That is funny how they put that; it made me chuckle. Welcome to some of our thoughts about time.

"Time keeps on ticking, ticking, ticking into the ocean." They keep repeating this in my head over and over. This is a change from the Steve Miller Band song "Fly Like an Eagle." The original line is about time slippin' into the future. It's interesting that the words were changed, and I am trying to understand what it means and why they changed the words.

Time is an illusion, created as a way to measure, keep track and give people a sense of accomplishment. What does measuring time really do as there really is no such thing as time as we understand it?

Humans need to go inward as you all have a sense and knowing when things need to be done, when to eat, when to rest, when to withdraw. You may fight against time due to deadlines, pressures needing to achieve. This can produce dis-ease in the body. If you do not learn to listen to your own rhythms, this is where illness, exhaustion, depression and anxiety can grow and fester.

Time was a construct to measure how the sun moves, daylight and nighttime. Time is a way to control deadlines, sleeping, and eating. Why does the world have different time zones? Why isn't the world on one time zone? Yes, that may mean A.M. is dark for some and light for others. It is just interesting to think about how easily we just accept things without questioning why they exist. Time is just one of them.

Time is vast and just keeps going; there really is no beginning and no end, just space and time. This is why we changed the words to *ticking into the ocean* to talk about the vastness of time. When and why did humans become so obsessed with time, measuring time, etc.? What do these guideposts really mean? You have been so conditioned to believe and trust certain things, but what if these things really do not exist in the big picture? What if your own time clock and knowingness are more important? When you hear the word *time*, what does it bring up for you?

In some of my other books, I have talked about how language is coded with symbols. We need to look beyond what is right in front of us and start to take the eagle's eye view. Shifting perspective is where all change comes from. When you can see or know things differently, then they will be. Has anyone noticed how much time is speeding up? If we think about time as a constant, how is that possible? The same unit of centuries, decades, years, months, days, hours and seconds feels different at different times. Interesting.

We come now to help you awaken--to help you be the multidimensional being you are while still in the human suit. Enjoy this journey. In the grand scheme of things, being incarnated is just the blink of an eye. See the bigger picture. Trust that there is more out there and in there than you think.

All lifetimes are happening simultaneously. How do you explain this with your current concept of linear time? Think bigger; start to see how connected you really are.

Questions:

What does the concept of time mean to you?

Do you feel like time is speeding up lately?

Are you driven by time and deadlines?

Do you trust your own rhythms?

My First Presentation

This section is brought to you by Jesus, Archangel Metatron and Ashtar of the Galactic Federation of the Light. This section is being brought to you without commercials or fillers. They are just cracking up; they think this is hysterical.

The first presentation I was ever asked to give was at the Edgar Cayce Society local branch. I remember being so excited that I was asked to give my first presentation. I knew who Edgar Cayce was, but not in any kind of detail, so I did some research. I ordered several books, and when I opened one of the books to a photo of the human heart and lungs, I froze. I remember thinking to myself, "Isn't it cool that a reminder of who we really are was left inside?" The photo of the heart and lungs looked like a body with wings, a reminder that we were all angels.

There is so much encoded in us: our physical structure (human body) and especially our DNA. We may never fully understand the scope, no matter how long we study. To be honest, I do not think we are fully meant to understand. I do not believe this is something we could ever wrap our physical minds around. I believe we are meant to look at the magnificence of who we are and what we are fully capable of being and doing and put that out into the world.

How do you add your unique note to the symphony that we all create? How does your light shine and connect to the light grid of the Earth? I think these are really important questions to start asking ourselves, not how much money do you have or what possessions do you own? We are here at this time to move away from the ego and the third chakra of power and into the heart and intuition. Are you ready to take this leap?

What comes up for you when you think about telepathy? Do you get scared? Are you excited? Is it something you dread? What are you afraid may be discovered? With everything connected through the web, there really is no place to hide. Eventually, everything comes out in the open. This is where we are moving– more of a connected consciousness.

This is why the current generation is fluent and able to use AI. They see, know and feel the possibilities and the bigger picture. They came in wired for where we are going, not where we are. In older generations, this often brings up fear. Maybe a way to think about it is that older generations helped bring the light and the way for the current generation. We all played and continue to play our parts.

They are showing me scenes from the movie *Whale Rider*. My interpretation is that the young girl knew her role, but no one believed it was her and that she was capable until she did what they never expected. Then she was able to take her place. Maybe we need to have more compassion and start to see and feel our world differently. Maybe it is time to start celebrating the differences instead of being in fear. Maybe it is time to get out of the groupthink and start to think and be authentic to your beliefs and sense of what is truth.

Questions:

Is it hard for you to use your voice and speak your truth?

Do you get easily swayed by information from other people?

Are you able to stand in your truth?

Ascended Masters, Angels and Light Beings

If the title doesn't say this already, this section is being brought to you by the Collective.

We, the Ascended Masters, Light Beings and Angels communicate through this one frequently. She can hold our collective energy as well as our individual energy signatures, depending on what humanity is working on or what we are choosing to share.

This one works a lot with Jesus, Metatron, Maitreya and Ashtar of the Galactic Federation of the Light; at least, these are the ones that come through more frequently.

When this one was stressed at a job situation years ago, Vishnu and his bird of prey, Garuda, went to work with her every day to help protect her and keep the darkness of others' plots at bay.

There are times Mother Mary, Kuan Yin, Mary Magdeline, Isis and the Earth Mother come in to give messages, educate and bring certain frequencies back to or incorporate into the Earth. We are all here to support, no matter what you believe in or who you feel called to work with.

So many come to her when she is open, as she is more of a clear conduit/channel. She just gets out of the way, receives the message and passes it along. That is rare in humans as they may get caught in the illusion of the human mind and the message needing to make rational sense of having a meaning for them.

If you can free yourself from the shackles of the human mind and constructs, all is possible, and you are capable. This is why there is a resurgence in meditation, retreats, yoga, energy work, etc. So many are looking externally for the connection, when the connection is inside and has been all along. Go within, not outwards, and you will receive all that you need to live and thrive.

For some reason, they are showing me Santa's workshop. Since I just talked about not tweaking the message, I'm just going to share what I am getting. By the way, they are all laughing because I grew up Jewish in this lifetime and cannot understand why they picked Santa's workshop to use as an example. In all seriousness, there will be many who relate to this analogy and it means something to them. Santa's workshop invokes an element of light, laughter, joy, merriment and happiness. We need more of this in our world right now. There needs to be a shift in the human condition/paradigm. Being human and in physical form is a gift so many souls/beings want to have. Everyone wants to be here right now at this time of great shifting and consciousness explosion. So many are cheering us on from the sidelines, encouraging us to awaken and be who we are designed to be. Know you are supported, loved and cherished as you see the possibilities of who you really are.

Questions:

Do you resonate with certain Archangels or Ascended Masters?

Are you drawn to certain colors or frequencies?

Do you often feel energy around you?

Message from My Younger Self

Wake up to who you really are.

It is time to rock the World.

Think of this July 4th as your personal Independence Day.

As you hear the fireworks tonight, remember you are a firework.

A divine spark.

A Light.

Laugh and play more and find more joy.

You know so much – let it out.

Have as much faith in yourself as I do in us.

Don't be concerned about naysayers.

We have got this.

Go forth and prosper.

-Younger Me 7/4/24

When I was re-reading this message completed with the activity of writing a letter to yourself in your non-dominant hand, leftover from my days as a therapist, I was dumbfounded. There in the first line was the name of my previous book and this book. I had not realized this until now. Over a year ago on some level, I knew that I was writing two books close together.

Sometimes we get messages and guidance in ways that we are not even aware of. This was one of those times. I had the information all along, I was just not conscious or aware of it yet.

So interesting when you stop to think about that.

After I found this information, I was wondering what else I had known and had not realized that I had known before it became conscious.

Thanks, Archangel Metatron, for the assist and the nudge to look through some old journals and messages I had written.

This is why it is important to go back and reread things. As we move forward in our journey, things can have a whole new meaning. How many times have you had a reading where information was given to you that did not make sense at the time? Then months or years later you are like, wait, I was told that a while ago and it makes perfect sense.

I have also had this experience with books I am reading. I have started books and gotten about three chapters in and just couldn't go any further. Then a couple of years or months later, I will pick up the book again and won't be able to put it down. It was perfect what I was going through during that second attempt, and I was apparently not ready when I had tried to read it before.

We all have this ability, and I believe that sometimes we need to just give ourselves some grace and that things may not move as fast as we would like.

The last story I will share about this, is when I had my first Akashic record reading during my Opening to Intuition course. Some information was presented to me that I did not understand. Later, I finally understood the information that was presented 20 years earlier and how that shaped and impacted me in my life. I had several choices:

1. I could have beaten myself up saying how much of an idiot I was that I did not see the connection.
2. I could give myself grace.
3. I could be grateful that I had done my work and was able to appreciate and synthesize that information into my current consciousness.

I went with the last option. You cannot beat yourself up for what you do not know. Perception and awareness are key, and you need to be ready and willing to do the work to get there. The information about events or people does not change, but our perception and awareness of people and situations change. Nothing is inherently good or bad, the old way of thinking. Everything just is the lens we see it through is up to us.

Questions:

What messages have you gotten that you didn't understand at the time?

Looking back on some of the messages, how does it feel now?

Have you ever written a letter to yourself in your non-dominant hand?

When You Feel Like Hope Is Slipping Away

I don't know about you, but 2025 has been a very intense year with so many souls transitioning and people having injuries. It feels like humanity is losing the battle of fighting for consciousness and light and a new way of being. I was reminded of this yesterday when I was doing my friend Jim's *Drop the Needle* podcast. He said something like, "What do you do when you feel like there is no hope or that things are not going to get better?"

I had not really given this much thought, as I had been guided to believe that we have got this, that humanity can make the shift to the fifth dimension. His earnest question made me stop and think, "Is this the end of human consciousness again? Are we at a point of no return?"

I have got to be honest; it makes me very sad to think about this and even entertain this thought process. With that said, there are so many losing faith, losing hope with every choice that seems to show that humanity wants to stay stuck, does not want to move beyond this. At least that is how it appears if you watch the news or social media feeds.

Behind this thought, there are many steadying humanities, many helping for the day that is coming where human consciousness will make a new choice and not wish to be stuck in duality or the third dimension anymore. It is still in the timeline; it is still a possibility.

One of the things I have been told by my spirit team is that there may end up being two Earths, at least vibrationally: one that is stuck in the third dimension and then one on the same planet that vibrates higher in the 5th dimension. It is like layers. Both can exist at the same time.

Sometimes, change is just a shift in perspective, about believing that the unimaginable is possible. As long as there are warriors of the light fighting or encouraging others to raise their vibration, then it is still possible. As long as there is a flicker of light no matter how small or infinitesimal it is, there is hope, there is a chance. Do not count out humanity. If we all rise together and all dream a new reality into consciousness, then it is possible. The Collective is working with all those awake to the dream within the dream to help others start to wake up from the layers of deep sleep to see the game or choices that they still have. We are still being given an opportunity to balance growth with consciousness and heart. I hope that we all take advantage of this opportunity.

We are held and loved by so many forces on both sides of the veil. Do not lose your faith or sense of wonder or awe. These are going to be important to make the shift to change, to be open. We have got you. We can all do this together. The Collective helped me to write this section and to put into simple words very complex issues and vibrational patterns that exist, that some are aware of but not all. The goal is to have the majority of humanity awaken in this amazing time and to take back our sovereignty. You have all got this: be, breathe and believe.

Questions:

What does your faith look like?

Do you believe in miracles and possibilities?

Do you believe that humanity can shift?

What can you do to support the shift?

Connection and Grounding

Sometimes Archangel Metatron and Maitreya are really pushy, and this is one of those times. I woke up this morning, knowing that I had been traveling all night, working on the other side and was physically tired as I did not get much physical sleep. That aside, I woke up thinking about the grid of humanity and how we are all connected. It is imperative that all of our lights come up on the grid in order for human consciousness to shift.

Sometimes I see the grid of humanity as ley lines covering the earth and each human being as a point of light. I can see where the issues are and the dark spots that need to be lit up. The grid needs to be active; we need to take our place as the human race we are meant to be. This is the time. There is no more waiting to see what happens or how things are going to be resolved. We are who we have been waiting for. Now is the time.

There is still time for the Earth and humanity to shift, and it will take as many of us who are willing to do the work and see beyond the veil.

What is real? This is a question I get asked all the time. We are creating our reality, and we can create a more loving one if we are willing to let go of the illusions and control that has been keeping humanity stuck for eons, just like in the *Matrix* movies.

It is going to be important to stay grounded as we shift, this is always a challenge. I say *challenge* because as you continue to shift the way that you need to ground will change. Sometimes, we try and continue to ground in the same ways we always have and as the energy in and on Earth changes the way we ground may need to as well.

The Earth Mother holds all of us. The analogy I was shown was balloons tied together, each separate and forming a whole like the ocean is one body of water yet made up of millions of individual drops. This is humanity. We are one consciousness, yet millions of different possibilities.

Another way to think about it is we are a huge, massive tree. Our individuality is the branches, but we cannot have the whole tree without all of its parts: roots, trunk, branches, etc. We are all a part of the tree of life, separate and yet connected.

All of our gifts and essences are of equal importance. We are a symphony and to a trained ear, we can hear each of the instruments and together make a harmonious sound.

Questions:

What does grounding mean to you?

Do you have a grounding practice?

Do you feel grounded when in nature?

Section Three:
Beings and Messages

Unicorns, Unicorns, Unicorns

I have always had a special connection to the unicorns. I have even written a children's book featuring healing unicorns called *Be Free to Be Yourself: The Magical Unicorn*, a story about how being different and accepting yourself can ultimately change how others view you.

I have had the privilege and honor of channeling unicorns for years, and they want me to talk about the connection between the seen and unseen worlds.

Unicorns exist, just not currently in the third dimension as the frequency is not high enough for them to physically manifest at this time. They currently reside in the 7th dimension as they are 7th dimensional beings. Unicorns bring joy, happiness, luck, wishes, healing and even protection at times.

When I meditate, I will often connect with the unicorns and receive love, compassion and friendship, much like equine therapy with horses in this dimension.

Sometimes when I am driving, I will have a herd of unicorns forming a shield around my vehicle. This happened the other day when I was driving home from a short trip in the rain. The unicorns stayed with me the whole trip, guided my way, and protected me. You could say it was like Rudolph guiding Santa's sleigh. The unicorns wanted to make sure I arrived safely at home as I was very upset, anxious and emotional about a good friend's cancer diagnosis I had just heard.

While the unicorns were with me, I had the most unusual experience. (Okay, for me it is not that unusual, but for you, the reader, it may be.) When I shared this experience with friends, I understood just how powerful and magical it was and how fortunate I am to have this experience.

I found myself in two planes of existence at the same time. I was driving on the rain-filled highway with a lot of trucks, and I was transported to a multidimensional highway of light. My spirit team was being funny, and the unicorns love when we are laughing and in joy, making it easier for them to come through. This is why they connect with children a lot. I started hearing the AC/DC song "Highway to Hell"; however, the words were changed to "You are on the highway to Light." They sang it like AC/DC would, just with different words. I was laughing at this point! Who turns the song "Highway to Hell" to "Highway to Light"?

I have to say when I arrived home safe and sound, I first thanked the unicorns and then realized what a profound experience I'd had. I was in the seen world and unseen world at the same time. Both existed simultaneously. Although I was still anxious about hearing more about my friend's health and what I could do to support her, I had a profound sense of peace, calm, connection, knowingness, love, compassion and wisdom all at the same time. I could hold all of these emotions simultaneously. I was starting to realize exactly what the human suit is really capable of and how easy it is if we just surrender and forget what we thought was true and to surrender to what is possible.

Sometimes I get my best information while driving. I have gotten downloads a lot while I am on highways over the years. I am still changed from this experience. What would Earth and humanity be like if we could all see the world from this perspective? What a world it would be.

It begs the question: Why can't we start to see the world from a sense of love, calm, peace and knowingness, bring this into the third dimension, and anchor it so that everyone can have these kinds of transformational experiences?

This section was written in conjunction with the unicorns. I am so blessed to be able to connect and communicate with them.

When it is the darkest and it feels like all hope is lost and you don't know what direction to go, remember even during these times, there is joy, there is hope and laughter, and lighter times are possible. Something I am reminded of by the unicorns to put here in an acronym for *hope*: **h**earts, **o**pening, **p**erfectly, **e**very time. Sometimes it just takes faith.

We, the unicorns, come and play during these trying times. Some on the planet now are great healers and are connected to the 7th dimension where we currently exist. Something to think about is these healers do not have horns in this lifetime like we unicorns do. The energy is being transmitted through their hands and heart. Keep this in mind. Healing comes in a lot of different forms.

You can have great healing abilities. However, if you are not pure of heart and intent, then it does not have the same resonance. The heart and hands need to be in balance and alignment. Joy lives in the balance of heart, hands and intent.

The Unicorns

Questions:

Do you like unicorns?

Do unicorns ever visit you in meditations or your dream time?

Do you feel a sense of joy, and happiness when you think about unicorns?

The Earth Mother

There are many changes happening on and within me. Just like humans I am going through changes. I have a rhythm, sequence and order I go through when I shift. I have shifted many times and will continue to evolve just as humans do. I am not stagnated. I am a living being and presence.

What you humans do affects me and changes me. As a humanity you need to remember that Earth is your home and what you do, how you live, and your recklessness affect both of us.

If you destroy me and continue to cause damage, you will no longer have a home as humans will cease to exist as I will become uninhabitable and unstable.

Your home is not just your house, your family and within you; it is also on me and a part of me. We are connected, and it is time for you to start to show some respect for me and yourself.

Yes, I have many resources and as you deplete them, they will no longer exist, I cannot just make more to suit you and your needs. We are in this together, and we need each other more now than ever.

Thank you for taking the time to think about the impact you have and what you can do individually to keep both of our homes intact.

-The Earth Mother

Questions:

What can you do to honor your relationship with the Earth Mother?

How can you care for the planet we all call home?

Can you send energy to the Earth Mother?

The Collective

To Humanity:

It is time. The world is shifting so fast that many humans are having a hard time staying focused and grounded.

We are here to help, hold space and are sharing with those who can access our frequency and vibration. We come in love, friendship, and bring knowledge and wisdom for you to move forward. You humans are not alone; you never have been alone. Wake up from the dream and start to trust and be who you really are.

Many are waking up at this time. We hoped Covid would bring the shift, and it did for a little while. Then everyone went back to sleep once the crisis was over. We need you to stay awake and be part of the shift.

The old ways do not work–it is time to let them go. Shift into the new matrix that is all around you. Full moon days like today as this one is channeling us make it easier as the veil is thinner and more knowledge is attainable.

Turn your light on; it is needed. We know these messages are similar. Each one is coded with a slightly different frequency and vibration to reach as many people as possible.

Each human has their own resonance and frequency; therefore, the messages coming through each have a different vibration coded into it. It is important for each of you to figure out what your own truth is and what you believe in. This one channeling has always believed this and never tried to push her beliefs onto anyone else. This is vital. As each person has free will, they need to decide for themselves what they believe to be true.

So many of you do not believe in yourselves or think you do not have value or merit. This is untrue, a way to stay stuck and controlled. It is like a large part of humanity is just a void going through the motions. We wish more for you and for you to start to believe in yourself and what is possible. You are each a spark of the Divine and carry your own light. It is time to turn it on and let it shine. You are all capable. Believe, breathe, have trust and faith.

-The Collective

Questions:

What do you feel?

Does it resonate?

If so, where in your body do you feel it?

Do you have a knowing?

Jesus and Maitreya

Dear Ones:

In life sometimes what you as humans perceive as the worst thing that can happen to you has been put in your path to move you in a different direction, a change of course so to speak. This obstacle is to help move you past the fear of moving in a different direction. It's course correction by your spirit team. They are laughing again; they think that is funny. They are talking about how seriously we take everything. Life on earth is a heartbeat: lighten up, see the joy and beauty all around you. Now back to the message.

Sometimes you as humans get in your own way, and situations, experiences, events happen to propel you in a different direction. It is all a matter of perspective and how you perceive the path and events.

Start to see the big picture, not the individual situations. Your life is a tapestry of colors, experiences and people. How do you want to weave it? Your tapestry is the story of who you are, your soul growth.

Start to see the majesty of life. Trust, have faith, persevere and know you are okay, and everything is unfolding as it is meant to.

Free will is about choosing which event, situation, or friendship is going to fulfill your contract and allow your soul to grow. Each experience is a choice, a possibility, not right or wrong. You learn and you grow. This is why you are on Earth, sometimes called school. The only thing that is predetermined is what lessons the soul wanted to achieve in this lifetime. How you get there is completely up to you in the human suit.

-Jesus and Maitreya

Questions:

Do you feel stuck?

Do you have a hard time making decisions?

There is no right or wrong with decisions, only growth and movement. Could this shift in perspective help you?

Epilogue

It is so interesting, as I finished the writing portion of this book about three weeks ago. I had been struggling to write this epilogue. Usually, this part just flows after I have completed all the sections, but not this time. Then it hit me. I am struggling because this is not the end of the story; it is just the end of this book. There is more to say, to experience and explore I have been told by my spirit team but now is just not the time to share it. I often feel I get messages and downloads and then am instructed, "No, wait; it is not time." I feel like my life is an endless loop of "hurry up and wait." I am sure others feel that way as well.

I would like to thank all of you for taking this journey with me. I hope this book has provided you with some food for thought, has maybe shifted your way of thinking and seeing the world. We all need to be who we really are and to take our place if we want to shift human consciousness.

Until the next book and next piece of the puzzle drops in.

Good Journey, Fellow Traveler!

About the Author

Gail Alexander, No-Nonsense Intuitive, Life Coach, Author, Speaker, Medium, Therapist, and Multidimensional Artist.

How often have you heard, "The truth is out there" or "If you want answers, look within"? And how many times did you respond that you didn't have the first clue what to do with statements like that?

That's where Gail Alexander comes in. She actually does know. Gail knows how to access information that you haven't learned to find for yourself.

Gail has since studied many different healing traditions, including ARCH (Ancient Rainbow Conscious Healing), Angelic Healing Fire, DNA Theta Healing, EFT, Reiki, and Quantum Touch. Intuitively, she assesses which to use with each client and may draw on and interweave aspects of each. She is becoming especially well-known for the extraordinarily beautiful, energy-infused mandalas she channels.

One day we will all step into our ability to access the energy around us. Until then, whether it's physical, mental, emotional or spiritual healing, questions about those who have transitioned, or if something is out of balance in your life, Gail Alexander is honored to be of service to you and others looking for answers they feel are just out of their reach.

www.gail-alexander.com

https://linktr.ee/GailAlexander

Other Books by Gail Alexander

- *Mandalas Created for the World & Humanity*
- *Energy Mandalas of Crystals & Stones*
- *Healing Energies Mandala Coloring Book*
- *I Don't Know How I Know . . . I Just Know*
- *I Still Know What I Know*
- *Sharing What I Know*
- *Jesus and the Jewish Girl*
- *Bree Free to Be Yourself: The Magical Unicorn*
- *The Great Awakening of 2020: A Mandalic Journey*
- *Mandala Coloring Book: Healing Edition*
- *Mandala Coloring Book: Dolphin, Unicorn and Mermaid Edition*
- *Mandala Coloring Book: Winged Being Edition*
- *Wakey-Wakey, It's Time! Humanity, Pay Attention*

www.ingramcontent.com/pod-product-compliance
Lightning Source LLC
Chambersburg PA
CBHW051223120626
46547CB00013B/1478